Copyright 1993, 2012 Dr. Mickey Frazier, Sr.
All rights reserved. No part of this book can be
reproduced without the prior permission
of the author and publisher.

Published by Frazier Publishing
P.O. Box 363835
North Las Vegas, NV 89036-7835

ACKNOWLEDGMENTS

The work of Court Reporter Pam Lewis was brilliant. Her dedication and attention to detail was awesome. Thanks again!

DISCLAIMER

This book is sold with the understanding that the author and publisher are not engaged in offering legal advice. The purpose of this book is to complement and supplement other text on the subject. You are urged to read any and all available information and learn as much as possible before starting. Every effort has been made to make this book as accurate as possible. Use this book as a general guide and be sure to check the laws and regulations in your area before starting. The author shall have no liability and responsibility to any person or entity, with respect to the loss or damage caused, or alleged to be caused, directly or indirectly by the information contained in this book. This book is not affiliated with any government.

TABLE OF CONTENTS

CHAPTER 1	WHAT IS SMALL CLAIMS COURT?
CHAPTER 2	WHAT ARE WE TALKING ABOUT?
CHAPTER 3	WHICH CASES ARE HANDLED?
CHAPTER 4	HOW MUCH CAN I SUE FOR?
CHAPTER 5	CAN I COLLECT OUT OF STATE?
CHAPTER 6	SECRETS TO VICTORY
CHAPTER 7	EUROPEAN SMALL CLAIMS PROCEDURE

HOW TO WIN IN SMALL CLAIMS COURT AND COLLECT

INTRODUCTION

Author, producer and publisher Dr. Mickey Frazier, Sr., explains a simple action-oriented plan for recovering monetary damages through the small claims court system. Through his detailed study and court battles against individuals, small companies and major corporations, Mickey offers rational logical guidance that will save you time as well as frustration in recovering your money. You've tried to get them to pay. You've told them verbally and written a demand letter, all to no avail. It's time to fight back. Small claims court allows us to fight back and play the game in a big way. Anyone can receive monetary compensation if you utilize the small claims court system. I will remind you throughout my book that states vary in many aspects of the system, including the courts that handle the cases. Some states call it "People's Court." Others call it "District Court." A few call it "County Court." It may be called "Circuit Court," "Municipal Court," "Justice Court," "Magistrate Court," or" Justice of the Peace." In Europe it's called Small Claims Procedure". Regardless of the variation it means "Small Claims Court."

I'm in the real world, some people try to steal from me, and I stop them, frequently, take them to court. I love a good lawsuit. It's fun.

~Alan Alda

CHAPTER 1
WHAT IS SMALL CLAIMS COURT?

There is no person in this room whose basic rights are not involved in any successful defiance to the carrying out of court orders.

~Dwight D. Eisenhower

What is Small Claims Court? It's the least expensive and easiest way to obtain redress for no criminal disputes. In a day when civil suits take years to resolve, chances are good that you can get into small claims court within 60 days and win using my techniques. In many states it will be under 30 days. It is underutilized in most states. As I talk to people across the country I am convinced that many people just do not know how to go about it. The court system is complex and intimidating. Many think you have to be a lawyer to understand it. But you do not have to have any special training to work your way through the small claims court. I hope that I can assist you with some of the doubt about you winning in small claims court. This book will explore the costs involved with filing a claim. We will analyze the different cases handled by the small claims court. We will look at how much you can sue for. I will give you tips and I will discuss many other aspects of small claims court.

CHAPTER 2
WHAT ARE WE TALKING ABOUT?

"He'll let the lawsuit do the talking."

~Mother Jones

We are talking about a swift and simple process. You can file in the city where damages occurred or the closest small claims court. We're going to the courthouse. We're going to fill out a piece of paper with the names, addresses and phone numbers of you and the defendant along with the amount you're going to be suing for and then we're going to go home and then wait for a court date. The form is mainly your statement of the facts involved in the case. It can be brief. They failed to pay on an agreement. It's that simple. It's easy. We're talking about a hearing that may even be held on a weekend or an evening. It doesn't necessarily have to be held on a 9 to 5 Monday through Friday. The technical rules of evidence and legal procedures are relaxed. When I say "relaxed" I do not mean bring your dinner or your pet to court with you. The Judge simply hears both sides of the case and allows any evidence or the testimony of any witnesses that either party produces. Most claimants save lawyer fees and represent themselves. In fact some states do not permit lawyers in such courts unless they are representing themselves. You can save the lawyer fees and representing yourself.

Let's take a closer look and see what claims are handled by the small claims court system. A small claims court will address almost any grievance that can be resolved by money demands. If something has harmed you, your property or your money, take a look at small claims court. What about a breached contract or agreement? What about defective merchandise? Let's just use the latter as an example. There are people and companies that will not give you a refund under any circumstances.

One key to collecting on defective merchandise is to make sure that you sue the right person or business. For instance your cell phone is broken. You take it up the street to John's Cell Phone Shop. John puts a defective part on your cell phone. You sue John but later you find out that ABC Corporation owns John's shop. Even though John owns all the parts and equipment in ABC Corporation your judgment is not collectible out of the corporation's assets. You must sue where the assets are. You cannot necessarily sue the name on the business or the person you assume owns the business. Just because the name is on the wall does not mean the person owns it. The Department of Consumer Affairs and local business licensing agencies may be able to assist you with your homework on that matter.

The point I'm making is don't let it slide. What about the landlord who does not return the security deposit? What about the tenant who destroyed the rental units? What about the tenant that owes you past due payments? What about a minor accident whereby repairs were agreed to be paid? What about the repairman who did a poor job and made unnecessary repairs? People will put you off forever when it comes to your money. They'll put you on hold for years if you'd let them. There are hundreds of scenarios. We could go over them all day. The big companies and corporations do not like small claims court. I do not advise this, but on behalf of my son I had to sue the CEO of a major corporation. Generally you cannot sue the owner of a corporation unless you have a personal claim against the individual that is separate from his or her business activities.

For the most part it's not collectible but it brings attention to the problem. If he or she is any type of boss he'll get it taken care of. This company broke a written agreement and my son was deeply hurt. The sheriff served the CEO at the company headquarters. When the sheriff serves the boss you get results. By the way, I do recommend that you use the sheriff to do the serving. People know that you're serious, and it's a lot easier with minimal cost.

Serving with registered or certified mail, a third party, or friend over the age of 18 is okay but there's something about a gun that gets people's attention. In my son's case within days we received what we were supposed to via special delivery and we received an additional five items. I believe we got their attention. Use your best judgment to decide if your complaint is serious enough for small claims court. Along with general damages, some states allow punitive damages and pain and suffering. Certain cases cannot go to small claims court. Cases such as divorce, adoption, and most court orders a small claims Judge will not hear any cases like that.

If someone is legally responsible and you want monetary compensation, small claims court is the place to go. This brings us to the word "small" a relative word. Some think of small when their bank account balances go down to $200,000. Others think of small when he or she goes to put that $5 pair of shoes on their credit card and the teller says, "Fine or Insufficient funds." I'm sure somebody knows what I'm talking about. I'm sure many of you know someone that I'm writing about. I will refer to filing fees of generally under $50.00 as small. Connecticut is on the high side with a $90 filing fee. Some states have filing fees based on the amount you are suing for. Check with your local small claims court clerk for fees.

CHAPTER 4
HOW MUCH CAN I SUE FOR?

"And if it be stolen from him, he shall make restitution unto the owner thereof."

~Bible

Let's get to the meat and potatoes here. I'm often asked, "Mickey, how much can I sue for? What is the max?" The amount varies from state to state. The limits are often revised upwards by state lawmakers. Once again, check with your local small claims court clerk for current limitations. Claimant maximums currently range up to $25,000 in some parts of Tennessee. Georgia and Delaware have limits up to $15,000. Most states have a range of $5,000 to $10,000. In Europe you can sue for less than EUR 2000. People are lobbying their state legislators trying to get their amount moved up. Remember to include your fees in your total amount of your lawsuit. Any proof of serving, if you miss a day's work, a day's pay from work, includes that also. Let the Judge say no. Include any expenses that you incur. Of course it will be up to the Judge to allow those or not. Let him or her be the Judge in the matter.

CHAPTER 5
CAN I COLLECT OUT OF STATE?

"We'd like to have this contract and this lawsuit settled. We were doing pretty good until we got to the money situation, but we've been stalled."

~Charles Richards

You can collect even if assets are out of state. Under the U.S. Constitution judgments are reciprocal from one state to another. If you have a judgment against an individual or a business in one state that has assets in another you can have the judgment registered in the state you wish to collect. The judgment is then viable in both places at the same time and if you can collect in either state. In regards to Europe you can collect from country to country.

CHAPTER 6
SECRETS TO VICTORY

"The greater our innocence, the greater our strength and the swifter our victory"

~Mahatma Gandhi

Let's go to the day of the hearing. You have your witnesses and relevant pictures, subpoenas, your proof of purchase, all the documents that you need. You can make two copies of your evidence and your proof of service and all your other documents; because the originals will go to the Judge. One set is for you and one set is for the defendant. That way everybody will be on the same page if the Judge makes reference to any of the documents. You're on time. You're ready to go. The claimant will present their case first. They present all the evidence. The Judge or the Judge pro tem likes all types of evidence that will support your case. It will make their job easier. It's very important that you be what I call the three C's. These are my three C's and they are courteous, concise and clear. Make sure your point is understood.

<u>Do not and I'll repeat this, do not interrupt the Judge, the defendant, or any of the witnesses while they are speaking.</u> Make notes if something is said that you wish to respond to. Respond to all questions the Judge asks you. You will have a chance to rebut anything that's said. You will get your chance. Avoid any excessive arm or body motions while speaking. Keep a calm and cool voice. Keep a fair attitude. You know a fair attitude's a must. You know, you're not expected to have a great attitude because you think that you've been wronged and you want your

money. You think you should have had your money. In addition, show that you know your case and rehearse what you're going to say to the Judge. The secret to winning is doing your homework and knowing your case. Oftentimes the loser will write a check after the Judge makes a decision. This happened to me in San Diego. It was a car accident case. A teenaged driver hit me. I had gotten three estimates and I showed the estimates to his father. His father was going to go ahead and pay me but decided to give his son a lesson. So I took him to court and show him some responsibility for his actions.

I sued him and won. His father later told me it was a valuable lesson his son would never forget. So far we've talked about the many advantages of small claims court. There are disadvantages in suing in small claims court. The major drawback is the jurisdictional limitations on the amount in which you can recover. Big claims require a big court, which requires a big wait and big money. Additionally the judgments are absolutely binding and you may not have a chance to appeal. This is it. In a state like New York the small claims court will allow appeals if you can show a grave injustice has been done. It's very difficult to say the least.

Another disadvantage is the judgment may not be collectible if you've sued someone with no assets. You are responsible for informing the local sheriff or marshal's office as to where to find the debtor's assets.

They will garnish wages and place liens against property but it's your responsibility to let them know where the debtor works or how they're getting their income or where they have property located. Real estate, bank accounts, business equipment, cars, stocks and bonds are few and collectible items. Do not become frustrated. You can collect if they have assets. Oftentimes you may say, "It's a waste." "It's not a waste."

Are you familiar with the term till tap or keeper? A till tap consists of a one time removal of all cash receipts from the business. In other words they go one day during the height of business just when they're just getting ready to close maybe a Saturday or something. The marshals remove all the receipts and money from the day to satisfy the debt. An effective keeper, which is a deputy from the sheriffs or marshal's office goes to the place of business and takes all the cash in the cash register that day and stays an additional 8 to 24 hours to collect all the money from all the other customers that come in. If your state offers this service its well worth the fee. It's very effective when it comes to collecting against the businesses.

A business can have its assets seized. It can be sold. Talk to the marshals or the sheriff's office for more details after you win your judgment and get a writ of execution against the business. The judgment can be good for as many as ten years. In general sheriffs and marshals will not go after stereos, televisions. Automobiles but tax refunds and wages are all open game. The collection on judgment varies from state to state. Your local small claims court clerk will know of actions that can be taken against the debtor. Collection agencies and lawyers may be of assistance in this matter. If all else fails, sell your judgment to a collection company for a fee. They will be happy to negotiate with you.

CHAPTER 7
European Small Claims Procedure

The European Small Claims Procedure was established in 2009 for matters less than EUR 2000. Small Claims Procedure matters usually take 30 days if the courts need no additional information. Your first step is getting the four different forms. Form A is your claim form. This is the most important form. Form B is the request by the court to complete or rectify claim from. Form C is the answer form and Form D is the certificate concerning a judgment in the European Small Claim Procedure. For more information and a guide to the European Small Claim Procedure go to www.ukecc.net

Please apply what you've learned today and you will be a winner! Justice will be done in your case. God bless you.

GLOSSARY OF BASIC LEGAL TERMS

A

Adjournment: is a temporary postponement to a case

Administrator: the person appointed to oversee an estate in the event that no will is written

Affidavit: A sworn written statement

Alimony: also known as "maintenance" and "spousal support", alimony is the money paid by one spouse to another following a divorce

Annul: to void

Annulment: is a legal decree stating that a marriage was not valid – not to be confused with "divorce"

Appeal: a request to a higher court to overturn the judgment of a lower one

Arbitration: a method of amicable dispute resolution

Arraignment: the initial appearance before a Judge in a criminal case – it is at this hearing that a defendant can enter a plea, ask to post bail, and, if the defendant cannot afford one, have a court lawyer appointed

Article of Incorporation: is a document filed with the state incorporating a limited liability company

Assignment: is the transfer of legal rights from one person to another – not the same as an **novation**, which is the transfer of legal obligations from one person to another

Award: a decision, usually by an arbitrator, in favor of a plaintiff or defendant, as the case may be

B

Bail: money paid to the court to guarantee the defendant's attendance at court at a later date. Money paid is more commonly known as a **bail bond**

Bankruptcy: a process governed by federal law where a person cannot pay bills when due and payable – chapter 7 and chapter 13 bankruptcy actions

Beneficiary: the person named as such in a will or insurance policy. A beneficiary may also be the equitable named person under a trust, where the legal owner is the trustee

Board of Directors: a group of individuals who run a company on behalf of the shareholders

Brief: a legal document that sets out the legal arguments in a lawsuit

Burden of Proof : is the duty, in law, to show, according to the facts, that the allegations to the lawsuit are either false or true – depending on the nature of the case

C

Capital Gain / Loss: the profit or loss, as the case may be, from the sale of an asset – such as your home. Ordinarily, but not always, capital gain will be taxed

Cause of Action: is the reason/grounds on which the legal action is being submitted/brought

Caveat Emptor: Latin meaning "buyer beware", this legal doctrine means that if you do not take due care when buying something, you cannot take your case before the courts

Certified Copy: also known as "certified true copy", this is a document signed as being a true copy of the original

Certify: to testify in writing

Class Action Lawsuit: is where two or more plaintiffs join together to bring a case against another

Collateral : is the security you agree to put down on a loan and which you will have to forfeit in the event that you cannot repay the loan – also known as "security"

Complaint: is a civil law action that initiates a lawsuit

Condition: are circumstances which are essential to the ascertain of a right; for example, it may be a condition to a loan that you give security, without giving security, you do not have the right to the loan

Conflict of Interest: means that you have competing interests in something that would make it difficult or impossible for you to fulfill your duty impartially

Consideration: is the thing, usually money, which you pay, under a contract, in exchange for getting something else

Contract: is a legal agreement entered into between two or more persons, known as "parties to the contract", whereby an offer is made and accepted

Costs: the sum awarded to the successful party to a lawsuit – and usually amount to the "costs", including legal fees, of having brought the case

Counsel: legal representative: lawyer or attorney

Creditor: someone to whom you owe money

Custodian: person appointed to manage and disperse funds on behalf of a child – unlike a trustee, a custodian is normally a court order persons

D

Damages: money paid to someone who has suffered injury or loss as a result of an action by a third party

Debtor: someone who owes money to a creditor

Decision: the verdict of a court in a case

Deed : a written legal document describing a piece of property and setting out the boundaries of that property

Default: is the failure to do something required of you under contract – an obligation. Ordinarily the obligation is to pay money, which is you do not pay, would mean you are in default of the contract

Defendant is the person who has charges to answer (criminal), or is being sued (civil)

Defined Benefit/Contribution Plan: essentially both a defined benefit plan and a defined contribution plan are forms of 401(k) retirement plans

Deposition is where a witness testifies under oath and you have pre-trial discovery to determine whether or not the deposition is in fact true

Discovery: the process, pre-trial, where each party to a case will ask for documentation and information relevant to their case

Dismissal: the termination of a case

Double Jeopardy: is the process of being tried twice for the same crime/offence

Due Process: is a legal doctrine that a person's trial proceeding be fair

E

Easement: a right given to one person to enter the property of another without having to ask permission each time – for example, the telephone/cable lines going into your home are an easement right

Encumbrance: is a claim on your property title – for example, a mortgage

Escrow: money paid into an account in the name of a third party which is then released once certain conditions have been fulfilled

Escrow Agent: the person appointed to look after the escrow account

Estate: all of the property of a deceased person

Evidence : documents, etc. that prove a claim as to facts

Executor: person named in a will to dispense the estate

Exempt Property: property which cannot form part of a bankruptcy lawsuit – usually work related property, such as the tools needed for work

Exhibit: document, evidence, provided to a court to support a claim

F

Fault: to be at "fault" means that you are to blame for something

Felony: a crime the nature of which is serious enough for you to spend one or more years in jail

Fiduciary Duty: is where you have an obligation to act in the best interest of a third party

Fine: punishment imposed for an offence

Foreclosure: occurs when a borrower cannot repay their debts and the creditor forecloses and sells the property – such as a house

Franchise: a business relationship whereby the owner of a business licenses others to use the name of his business

G

Good Faith: is to act honestly and without deception

Grand Jury: is a group of civilians convened to determine whether or not a criminal case has enough merit to proceed to trial

Grantor: the person who establishes a trust on behalf of the beneficiaries

Guarantee: a legal agreement under which a person agrees to guarantee the obligations of another

Guarantor: the person who provide a guarantee on behalf of another

H

Heirs : person entitled by law to inherit the estate of a deceased person

I

Implied: means to give the appearance – thus, you have "implied warranty", which means that you have given the appearance that there was a warranty, even if there was not one

Incompetency: to lack legal qualification or fitness to discharge a legal duty

Indemnity: to provide an undertaking to secure against loss or damages in the event of certain events – in other words: "compensation"

Injunction: a court order requiring you to stop doing something

Intestate: means to die without having left a will

J

Joint Custody: means that both parent have equal rights to a child following a divorce

Joint and Several Liability : means that you agree to be jointly and individual liable for a debt with another person

Judgment: the official decision given by a court

Jurisdiction: the court's authority to hear your case

Jury: group of twelve citizens charged with hearing your case

L

Lease: a legal agreement to lend/hire something to a third party.

Lemon Laws: laws that require manufactures to repair defective cars

Lessee: the person who hires something from a lessor

Lessor: the person who leases something

Liability: a duty or obligation for which you're a legally responsible

Lien: is a charge over your property = such as a mortgage

Limited Liability Company : is a business that has shareholders who are limited in liability to the contribution of the fully paid up share

Living Will : is a legal document that sets out a person's wishes should they become incapacitated

M

Maintenance: money paid to a spouse in the event of a divorce (also known as alimony)

Minor: a person under the legal age of consent (18)

Motion: a request made to a Judge asking him to rule on an issue of law

N

Natural Person: an individual – as opposed to a company or partnership

Negligence: a failure to use a degree of care

Notary Public: person authorized to witness documents

O

Oath: to swear to tell the truth

Order: direction (written or oral) of a court

P

Petition: written application to the court asking the court to take action on a specific matter

Plaintiff: the person who starts/commences a lawsuit

Pleadings: applies in civil cases and are the allegations made by each of the parties to the case

Power of Attorney: a legal document authorizing another to act on you behalf

Probate: the legal process where the court oversees the distribution of property under a will

Proceedings: the process of a lawsuit

Promissory Note: a written document under which a person promises to pay another money on a given date and pursuant to specified terms set out in the promissory note (also known as a "PN")

Q

Quid Pro Quo: is a Latin term which means you'll get something for having given something

R

Real Property: means land and all things attached to the land

Reasonable: means a level that an ordinary person would be expected to have, e.g. "reasonable care" means the level of care expected from a reasonable person

Reply: a plaintiff's response to a defendant's answer

S

Security Agreement: means a contract under which you agree to give security as collateral for a loan in the event that the loan is not repaid

Settlement: is an agreement or decision in a civil case

Shareholder: someone who hold shares in a limited company

Standard of Care: degree of care required to prevent injury to another

Statute of Limitations: is the period prescribed by law within which you have to file a lawsuit, otherwise you forfeit your right to being an action

Strict Liability: means that even if there is no proof of negligence, you can still be found guilty of an offence

Subpoena : legal order compelling you to appear in court

Summons: a legal document notifying you that a lawsuit has been initiated against you and how and where you must answer the claim

T

Testator: person who make a will

Tort : a civil wrong

Trust: property given to a trustee to manage on behalf of beneficiaries

Trustee: person charged with looking after property under trust

V

Verdict: formal decision by a jury/court on the facts of a case

W

Witness : a person who gives evidence in court under oath or who signs a document to testify/certify that the person who signed the document was who he claimed to be

Worker's Compensation: paid to a worker who suffers a work related injury or illness

Writ: a judicial order

www.ingramcontent.com/pod-product-compliance
Lightning Source LLC
Chambersburg PA
CBHW061521180526
45171CB00001B/279